P9-EGC-305

GOOD-BYE · BULLY MACHINE ·

Written by . . . . .
DEBBIE FOX and ALLAN L. BEANE, Ph.D.

free spirit
PUBLISHING®

Illustrated by DEBBIE FOX

Text copyright © 2009 by Debbie Fox and Allan L. Beane, Ph.D.
Illustrations copyright © 2009 by Debbie Fox

All rights reserved under International and Pan-American Copyright Conventions. Unless otherwise noted, no part of this book may be reproduced, stored in a retrieval system, or transmitted in any form or by any means, electronic, mechanical, photocopying, recording or otherwise, without express written permission of the publisher, except for brief quotations or critical reviews.

Free Spirit, Free Spirit Publishing, and associated logos are trademarks and/or registered trademarks of Free Spirit Publishing Inc. A complete listing of trademarks is available at www.freespirit.com.

Library of Congress Cataloging-in-Publication Data
Fox, Debbie.
  Good-bye bully machine / by Debbie Fox and Allan L. Beane ; illustrations by Debbie Fox.
     p. cm.
  ISBN 978-1-57542-321-0 (paperback edition)
  1. Bullying—Juvenile literature. I. Beane, Allan L., 1950– II. Title.
  BF637.B85F69 2009
  371.5′8—dc22
                                                                                        2008041025

Edited by Eric Braun
Cover and interior design by Natasha Kenyon

10 9 8 7 6 5 4 3 2 1
Printed in China
P17201208

Free Spirit Publishing Inc.
217 Fifth Avenue North, Suite 200
Minneapolis, MN 55401-1299
(612) 338-2068
help4kids@freespirit.com
www.freespirit.com

For my parents, who let me loose in their art studio.
Thank you for lighting the way.

For Tuck, because of all that has been and all that you are to me.

For Nina and Chad, and Nathan and Jenna.

It is your love that will always be my truest treasure.
—D. F.

I dedicate this book to my son, Curtis Allan Beane, who was bullied
in seventh grade and high school. It is also dedicated to my daughter,
Christy, my grandchildren, Emily Grace Turner, Sarah Gail Turner,
Jacob Allan Turner, and Jimmy Andrew Turner, and to my son-in-law,
Mike Turner. They have brought light into the darkness created by
Curtis's death. I hope this book, and those who use it, will bring light
into the darkness of students who are mistreated.

—A. L. B.

Acknowledgments

Thank you to Bonnie Swanson and Wendy Alexander for
their encouragement and ideas during the early life of this
book. We are grateful to Judy Galbraith, Steven Hauge, Eric
Braun, and Natasha Kenyon at Free Spirit Publishing for
the big hearts they have for children, and for caring enough
to make important books for them. Thanks also to Jen Arne,
Cordelia Anderson, and especially Carol Brandt-Fink for
their feedback.

Introduction for Grown-Ups

This book is about bullying, something most kids have experience with and many are traumatized by—and that's why we wrote it. We want to help kids and grown-ups understand how bullying can start, how it can grow, and how, if we act together, we can make it far less common than it is.

As educators and parents, we believe that kids deserve to feel safe, secure, accepted, and valued, whether they are at home, in their neighborhoods, or at school. That means being free from teasing, name-calling, harassment, threats, intimidation, violence, and fear. Whether you're an educator or parent yourself, this book can help you create that kind of experience for the kids in your life.

By sharing this book with kids and talking with them about bullying—and by taking their fears and reports of bullying seriously—you are doing a lot to help prevent the damaging effects of bullying. Activities in the back of the book help kids learn more about bullying and take a more active role in ending it. Finally, discussion questions, additional activities, and reproducible handouts are available as a free download at www.freespirit.com/bullyfree.

Thank you for your efforts against bullying.

Debbie Fox and Allan L. Beane, Ph.D.

A Note for Kids About "Bullies"

Bullying is a way of treating people that is mean and hurtful. People who bully aren't bad people. Their *behavior* is what's bad. **A person can learn to stop acting like a bully.**

In this book, we use the words "bully" and "bullies" to talk about kids when they show bullying behaviors. We do not mean that these kids are bad or that they will always be bullies. When you talk with other kids about bullying, don't call anyone a bully. Instead, talk about behaviors. Say, "I don't like it when you hit me or call me names. Stop it." This lets the person know exactly what you don't like. And it lets the person know that he or she can change and quit acting like a bully.

Calling people names, like "bully," can make them feel ashamed or angry. It might lead them to bully even more.

Imagine a scary machine.
This machine is loud and **powerful,** with spinning wheels and whirling blades. It's cold and mean and looks kind of dangerous.

**RUMBLE.
WHIRRR.
CHOMP.**

What would it feel like to be around this machine every day?

If you go to a school where there is bullying, maybe you know what it's like. A school with a **bullying problem** is not safe or fun. It seems like a place where feelings don't matter. Just like being around a powerful machine, being around bullying can be dangerous and scary. It can make you feel worried and **lonely.**

BULLYING
is when one or more people hurt someone's body, feelings, or even his or her things, on purpose. Bullying actions usually happen over and over. Bullying is trying to have power over somebody.

A school with bullying is like **a school that is run by a machine— the Bully Machine.**

The Bully Machine is made of lots of junky parts, and nasty things make it grow.

Do you know what kinds of things help the Bully Machine? One thing is **mean words.** Bullies use words to cause fear and pain. They might say things right to someone's face, loudly across a room or playground, or quietly behind a person's back.

Loud or quiet, **words are powerful.** Bullying words hurt, and they are remembered. They can make kids feel scared, ashamed, or embarrassed. They can make kids feel angry, sad, or lonely. Kids may feel lots of these things at the same time.

Here's more nasty stuff that makes the Bully Machine grow:

cruel actions.

That's when people do mean things with their bodies, like pushing, slapping, tripping, punching, and kicking. They might stand in the way or break things or take things.

Just like bullying words, bullying actions **hurt**. They are remembered.

With all that pain, the Bully Machine gets **bigger** and **stronger**.

Sometimes kids are bullied in other ways—**quiet or sneaky ways.**

These ways help the Bully Machine, too. People can bully by spreading rumors and lies. This can damage or **destroy** friendships.

People might use computers and phones to send hurtful messages. They might make mean faces, roll their eyes, tell jokes about others behind their backs, or try to get friends to turn against each other. Leaving someone out on purpose—that's bullying, too.

Sometimes, the person being picked on is the **last one to find out** about it, because it's done in secret.

Sneaky or quiet bullying is just as cruel as other kinds of bullying. It hurts just as much.

All kinds of bullying make the Bully Machine rumble along with its belly full of meanness.

So **who gets bullied,** anyway?

Lots of people. Sometimes kids get picked on because they look or act differently from other kids. They might be quiet in class, or act silly a lot. Sometimes bullies pick on kids who they think look weak or scared, like they won't fight back. But bullies will pick on **anyone** they can frighten, embarrass, or hurt.

Many kids who get bullied think it never happens to anyone else. They feel alone. But chances are you know someone who has been bullied today. **Maybe you** have been bullied yourself.

Bullying happens a lot, but there's **nothing okay about it.**

Kids who bully are often angry, sad, jealous, or just plain unhappy. Maybe adults in their lives are mean to them and they think **being mean** is normal. Maybe they don't know a better way to express their anger or sadness.

Some kids bully because they want to feel powerful. They like to control people around them.

Bullies tease and push and take and use. But they don't have to keep being bullies. With a little **help**, they can find better ways to act around others. **Try this:**

compliment them

ask them for help

offer help

invite them to play

show respect even if they're not respectful

14

12 13

A MEAN WRONG IS NOT GOOD

Sometimes **TEASING** is meant to be playful and fun, like when friends kid you about the peanut-butter-and-pickle sandwich you take in your lunch every day. Other times teasing is meant to be mean, like when someone tries to make you feel bad about the way you look. **When teasing hurts, it's bullying.**

Kids who bully might think they are being funny or cool. They might think the things they do are no big deal. They might say they are **only teasing.** But teasing can be hurtful even when it's meant to be fun. Teasing can be bullying.

Bullies sometimes believe the person they're bullying deserves it. But **nobody deserves to be bullied.**

Ever.

Anyone can bully—boys or girls, big kids or small kids, good students or kids who have trouble with school. But it's not always easy to tell **who's helping the Bully Machine** grow. Sometimes, kids who bully might be really nice to most other kids. They might act very nice around grown-ups, too. So nice, in fact, that the grown-ups might have a hard time believing those kids would ever pick on others.

Have you met anyone like that?

Most kids agree that **bullying is wrong.** Even if it doesn't happen to them, they don't like it. But many kids are afraid to do anything about bullying. They might be afraid they will get bullied if they say anything. They might be afraid of getting hurt or being called a tattletale.

They might think:

I'm just glad it's not me.

I feel sorry for that kid.

I wish there was something I could do.

When kids know about bullying but do nothing, the Bully Machine grows stronger.

Bullying doesn't happen without people who act like it is okay.

To **REJECT** people means to be mean or unfriendly to them. It means you do not accept them for who they are.

Instead of being silent, **what can you do about bullying?**

Remember that words are powerful. Words can be used to hurt, but they can also help **heal** sadness and silence the loudest, meanest person. You can use words to help shut down the Bully Machine.

Use **your voice** to:

SAY KIND THINGS TO THOSE AROUND YOU.

SAY YOU WILL RESPECT OTHERS AND NEVER REJECT THEM BECAUSE OF WHO THEY ARE.

SAY AND DO WHAT IS RIGHT, EVEN WHEN OTHERS DO NOT.

THINK...

IT DOESN'T
HAVE TO BE
this way.

To stop bullying, you might have to stick up for yourself or someone else by **telling a bully to stop.** If the bullying doesn't stop, tell an adult. Parents, teachers, principals, counselors, and other adults want to help kids be safe. They can only end the bullying when they know about it.

Reporting a bully is not tattling or snitching. Tattling or snitching are done just to get someone in trouble. When you report bullying, you are **helping kids** who need it. Maybe you're helping yourself.

Standing up to bullies—by telling them to stop or by reporting them to an adult—is being an **ally.** It tells bullies that their behavior is **not okay.** Doing nothing tells bullies that their behavior *is* okay,

just how the Bully Machine likes it.

IF YOU DON'T TELL,
WE WON'T
STOP.

shhh

When **many kids act together as one,** standing up to bullying can be a lot less scary. It can also work better to make the bullying stop. It's hard for people to keep bullying when everyone around them says what they're doing is wrong.

This is math that the Bully Machine hopes you never learn:
Lots of voices **added** together against bullying **equal** a place where the Bully Machine can't run.

When you **subtract** the hate and mistreatment, your school can be a happier place.

It all starts with **one** voice.
Then **add another.**
Then **add another.**
And **another.**

(Keep going!)

How ➕ does ➕ **your** ➕ school ➕ add ➕ up?

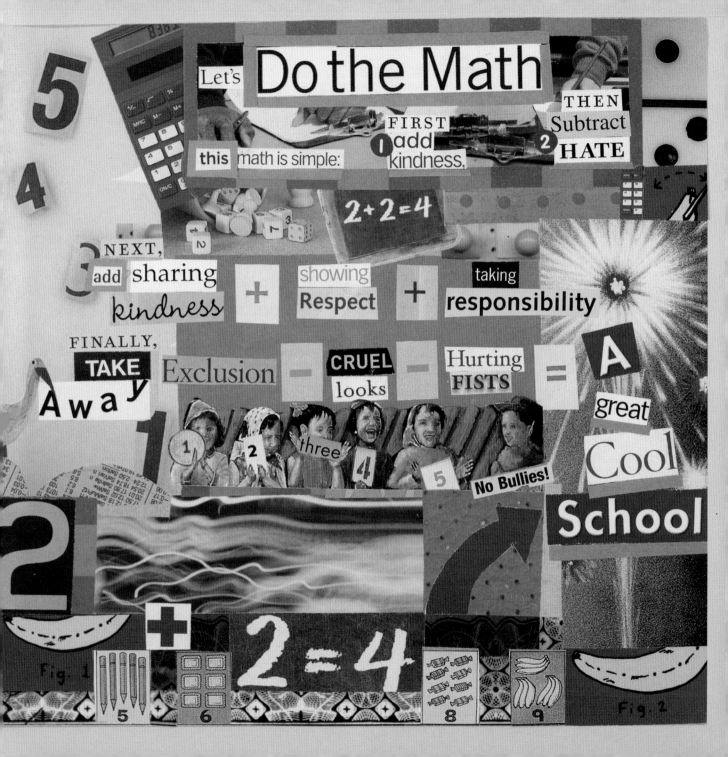

You probably like to be treated well. You want people to be nice to you and to give you a chance to show what a great person you are without judging or excluding you. You want to be accepted for who you are.

That's how others want to be treated, too. And that's what the **Golden Rule** is all about—treating others the way you'd like to be treated.

If you were being bullied and somebody else saw it happen, what would you want that person to do?

When the hurtful words and actions stop, the Bully Machine runs out of energy. It gasps and wheezes, it sputters and slows down.

It begins to fall apart.

CLUNK. CLANG. CRASH!

Usually, people feel bad when something mechanical breaks, like a furnace or bike. They think about how to get it fixed.

The Bully Machine is one machine that's better off broken!

Accept the challenge!

Team up with other kids and adults to **take a stand against bullying.**

- Respect everyone, no matter who they are.
- Make friends with someone who might need it.
- **Be an ally** to someone who is bullied.
- Be safe. If you feel unsafe around a bully, **get an adult's help.**

You can help make your school Bully Free.

When you choose to **act against bullying, you are choosing peace.** In a Bully Free school, all people choose to treat each other right.

They remember that choice every day.

Good-Bye, Bully Machine!

How to Be Bully Free
And Unplug the Bully Machine

If you're bullied . . .

- Bullies look for kids who seem scared or weak, so even if you don't feel confident, try to **appear confident.** Don't look at the ground, and do make eye contact with people you talk to. Speak up, and speak clearly. Sometimes a little humor can make you seem confident, too.

- Stick in groups if you can—bullies usually pick on kids who are alone.

- Avoid the bully.

- Stand up for yourself. If you feel safe, tell the bully in a firm voice to stop it. Be sure to make eye contact. Don't cry or act afraid.

- If the person doesn't stop, get help from an adult.

- If you don't feel safe, walk (or RUN!) away.

If you've been bullying others . . .

- People who bully are not bad people. It is their behavior that is bad. You can change if you want to.

- Treat people the way **you** want to be treated.

- If you start to feel upset or mad, **stop and think** before you act. Don't bully someone. Think about better choices you can make.

- Talk with an adult you trust about your strong feelings. Ask for help.

- Apologize to someone you have hurt (with actions or words). What can you do to make that person feel better? (Apologizing can help you feel better, too.)

- If you're trying to change, you don't have to promise to "never bully again." Instead, take it one day at a time: "I won't bully today."

If you witness (see) bullying . . .

- **Refuse to join in.**

- A person who knows about bullying is a **bystander.**
  A person who knows about bullying **and tries to stop it is an ally.**

- Tell the bully to stop. You can say things like, "Don't treat him that way!" and "Stop hitting her." Look for other allies to stand up with you.

- Be a friend to the person being bullied.

- If the bullying continues even after you speak up, it's time to get an adult to help.

Bully-Busting Activities

Learn more about bullying, spread the word about the Golden Rule, and feel good knowing you're helping break down the Bully Machine.

Draw a Bully Machine

Draw your own version of the Bully Machine. Use lots of details: What parts grow when people bully each other? What parts make noise, and what noise does it make? Can the machine move around? How? What falls off first when people start being nice to each other and following the Golden Rule?

Talk to an Adult About Bullying Experiences

Ask one or more adults you trust, such as parents or teachers, to talk about their experiences with bullying. Were they bullies, victims, bystanders, or allies? Or did they play different roles at different times? How did they feel during these experiences? Did their feelings change over time?

Write About Bullying

Write about an experience you had with bullying, as a bully, victim, bystander, or ally. Write what happened, what you did, and what happened next. How did you feel at the time? How did your feelings about the experience change, if at all?

Create Grocery Bag Swag

Ask a local grocery store manager if you can collect paper grocery bags from the store and decorate each bag with a Bully Free message—such as *Treat others the way you want to be treated*. Then return the bags to the store for them to use. Customers taking home groceries will appreciate the positive note.

Get Your School Involved

Ask your teacher or principal to help your school work toward being Bully Free with any of the following ideas. Use several ideas at once to build a powerful campaign against bullying.

Awareness Weeks. Hold a "No Gossip Week," when everyone in the school is asked to avoid gossiping for five days. You could design pledge cards, posters, and banners, and do skits and other activities. Another option is a "No Name-Calling Week." Ask everyone to avoid name-calling for five days. (This doesn't mean it's okay to gossip or call people names the rest of the year!) At the end of the week, conduct a survey to find out how people felt participating in the awareness week.

Decorations. Make Bully Free bulletin boards and posters to hang in classrooms, hallways, the lunchroom, the gym, the library, or all those places.

Announcements. Develop a series of anti-bullying messages to include with morning announcements. These could be songs, raps, poems, short skits, and brief reminders such as "Be an ally to someone who needs it."

Contests. Get your school to host one or more Bully Free contests. Ideas include contests for essay-writing, door-decorating, T-shirt design, poster design, or a poetry slam.

Skits. Work with your teacher and other students to develop anti-bullying skits to perform during assemblies and other school functions.

Welcoming Committee. Establish a "Welcoming Committee" for new students. The big-hearted kids on this committee show new students around the school, introducing them to students and staff and helping them feel like they belong. New students can often become the targets of bullying, so this is a very helpful idea for your school. And who knows, a new student might become your new best friend!

About the Authors

Debbie Fox is an elementary school arts and literacy educator and has created innovative, award-winning programs for children. A graduate of the Ontario College of Art in Toronto, Canada, Debbie is passionate about giving young people creative opportunities to express themselves. She and her husband live in Florida, close to their grown children. She has written two guidebooks for kids about her favorite state.

Allan L. Beane, Ph.D., is an internationally recognized expert on the topic of bullying. He has over 30 years' experience in education that include teaching special and regular education, directing a school safety center, and serving as vice president of a university. Author of the Bully Free® Program, Allan has trained staff in many schools on bullying and has served as an expert witness in criminal cases involving student mistreatment.

More Great Books From Free Spirit

The Bully Free Classroom™
Over 100 Tips and Strategies for Teachers K–8
by Allan L. Beane, Ph.D.

Allan Beane spells out more than 100 prevention and intervention strategies you can start using immediately. All are easy to understand and simple to implement; many require little or no advance preparation and few or no special materials. This solutions-filled book can make your classroom a place where all students are free to learn without fear—and you're free to teach because education, not behavior, is the focus. Includes 34 pages of reproducible handout masters.
176 pp., S/C, 8½" x 11", lay-flat binding. Grades K–8.

How to Be Bully Free® Workbook
Word Searches, Mazes, What-Ifs, and Other Fun Activities for Kids

Based on *The Bully Free Classroom* by Allan L. Beane, Ph.D., this hands-on, consumable workbook is full of engaging activities that help kids recognize bullying behaviors, understand that bullying is not acceptable, respond appropriately if they are bullied, know what to do when others are bullied, and more. Other activities focus on raising self-esteem, building assertiveness skills, managing anger, celebrating diversity, and showing kindness to others. The workbook may be used as a stand-alone, as a companion to *The Bully Free Classroom,* or as part of an anti-bullying effort already in place in a classroom, school, district, or youth group.
32 pp., illust., S/C, 8½" x 11". Grades 3–5.

Bullies Are a Pain in the Brain
written and illustrated by Trevor Romain

No one wants to be picked on, pushed around, threatened, or teased. Practical suggestions and humor help kids become bully-proof, stop bullies from hurting others, and know what to do in dangerous situations.
112 pp., illust., S/C, 5⅛" x 7". Ages 8–13.

Stick Up for Yourself!
Every Kid's Guide to Personal Power and Positive Self-Esteem
by Gershen Kaufman, Ph.D., Lev Raphael, Ph.D., and Pamela Espeland

Simple words and real-life examples help kids build genuine self-esteem, assertiveness skills, responsibility, and healthy relationships. A note to parents and teachers explores the "self-esteem backlash" and explains what self-esteem really is—and why kids today need it more than ever.
128 pp., illust., S/C, 6" x 9". Ages 8–12.

For pricing information, to place an order, or to request a free catalog, contact:

free spirit PUBLISHING®

217 Fifth Avenue North • Suite 200 • Minneapolis, MN 55401-1299
toll-free 800.735.7323 • local 612.338.2068 • fax 612.337.5050
help4kids@freespirit.com • www.freespirit.com